# 4-Chord Songbook

## Great Songs

**Babylon**
David Gray
page 4

**Early Morning Rain**
Gordon Lightfoot
page 7

**Danger! High Voltage**
Electric Six
page 10

**Dice**
Finley Quaye & William Orbit
page 12

**Don't Be Cruel**
Elvis
page 14

**Getting Away With It (All Messed Up)**
James
page 16

**Going Down**
The Stone Roses
page 18

**Keep What Ya Got**
Ian Brown
page 20

**Maggie May**
Rod Stewart
page 23

**La Bamba**
Ritchie Valens
page 26

**Red, Red Wine**
UB40
page 28

**Ruby, Don't Take Your Love To Town**
Kenny Rogers
page 30

**Stay Another Day**
East 17
page 32

**Sunday Morning**
Maroon 5
page 34

**Sweetest Thing**
U2
page 36

**So Young**
The Corrs
page 38

**Turn**
Travis
page 41

**Walk Of Life**
Dire Straits
page 44

**Woodstock**
Joni Mitchell
page 46

**Playing Guide**
page 3

This publication is not authorised for sale in the United States of America and/or Canada

**WISE PUBLICATIONS**
part of The Music Sales Group
London / New York / Paris / Sydney / Copenhagen / Berlin / Madrid / Tokyo

This *4-Chord Songbook* allows even beginner guitarists to play
and enjoy your favourite hits. The songs have been specially arranged
so that only 4 chords are needed to play all of the songs in the book.

The *4-Chord Songbook* doesn't use music notation. Throughout
the book chord boxes are printed at the head of each song; the
chord changes are shown above the lyrics. It's left to you,
the guitarist, to decide on a strum pattern or picking pattern.

Some of the arrangements indicate that a capo should be
used at a particular fret. This is to match the song to the key of
the original recording so that you can play along; otherwise the capo
is not needed for playing on your own. However, if the pitch of
the vocal line is not comfortable for singing (if it is pitched too high
or too low) you may wish to use a capo anyway; placing the
capo behind a suitable fret will change the key of the song
without learning any new chords.

Whatever you do, this *4-Chord Songbook* guarantees hours
of enjoyment for guitarists of all levels, as well as providing
a fine basis for building a strong repertoire.

Published by
Wise Publications
14-15 Berners Street, London W1T 3LJ, UK.

Exclusive Distributors:
Music Sales Limited
Distribution Centre, Newmarket Road, Bury St Edmunds, Suffolk IP33 3YB, UK.
Music Sales Pty Limited
120 Rothschild Avenue, Rosebery, NSW 2018, Australia.

Order No. AM994026
ISBN 978-1-84772-590-5
This book © Copyright 2008 Wise Publications,
a division of Music Sales Limited.

Unauthorised reproduction of any part of this publication by
any means including photocopying is an infringement of copyright.

Edited by Sam Harrop.
Printed in the EU.

www.musicsales.com

Your Guarantee of Quality

As publishers, we strive to produce every book to the highest commercial standards.

The music has been freshly engraved and the book has been carefully designed to minimise
awkward page turns and to make playing from it a real pleasure.

Particular care has been given to specifying acid-free, neutral-sized paper made
from pulps which have not been elemental chlorine bleached.

This pulp is from farmed sustainable forests and was produced with special regard for the environment.

Throughout, the printing and binding have been planned to ensure a sturdy,
attractive publication which should give years of enjoyment.

If your copy fails to meet our high standards, please inform us and we will gladly replace it.

## Relative Tuning

The guitar can be tuned with the aid of pitch pipes or dedicated electronic guitar tuners which are available through your local music dealer. If you do not have a tuning device, you can use relative tuning. Estimate the pitch of the 6th string as near as possible to E or at least a comfortable pitch (not too high, as you might break other strings in tuning up). Then, while checking the various positions on the diagram, place a finger from your left hand on the:

5th fret of the E or 6th string and **tune the open A** (or 5th string) to the note (A)

5th fret of the A or 5th string and **tune the open D** (or 4th string) to the note (D)

5th fret of the D or 4th string and **tune the open G** (or 3rd string) to the note (G)

4th fret of the G or 3rd string and **tune the open B** (or 2nd string) to the note (B)

5th fret of the B or 2nd string and **tune the open E** (or 1st string) to the note (E)

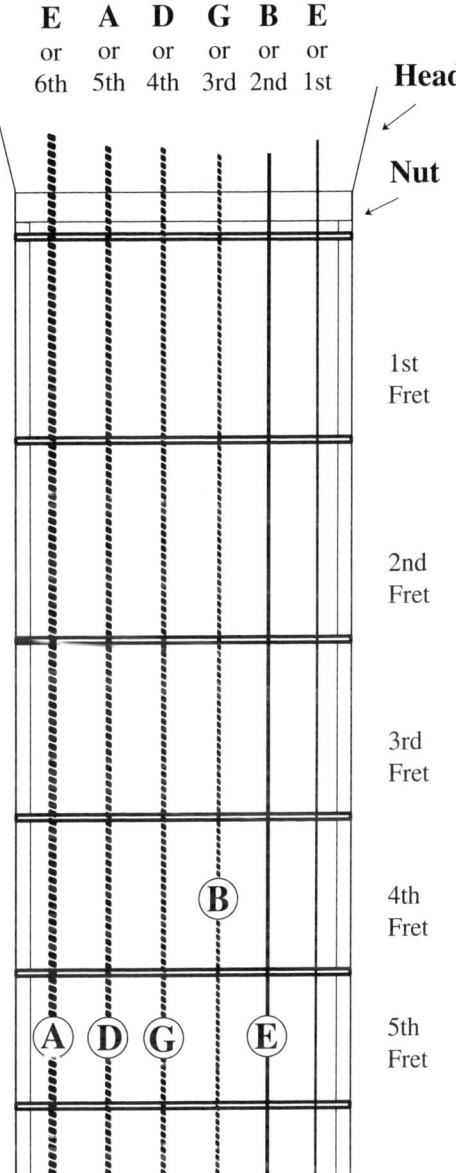

## Reading Chord Boxes

Chord boxes are diagrams of the guitar neck viewed head upwards, face on as illustrated. The top horizontal line is the nut, unless a higher fret number is indicated, the others are the frets.

The vertical lines are the strings, starting from E (or 6th) on the left to E (or 1st) on the right.

The black dots indicate where to place your fingers.

Strings marked with an O are played open, not fretted. Strings marked with an X should not be played.

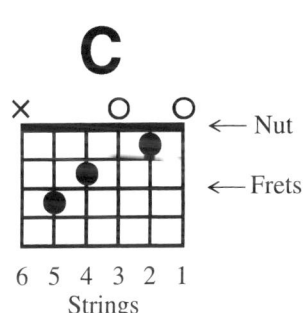

# Babylon

Words & Music by
David Gray

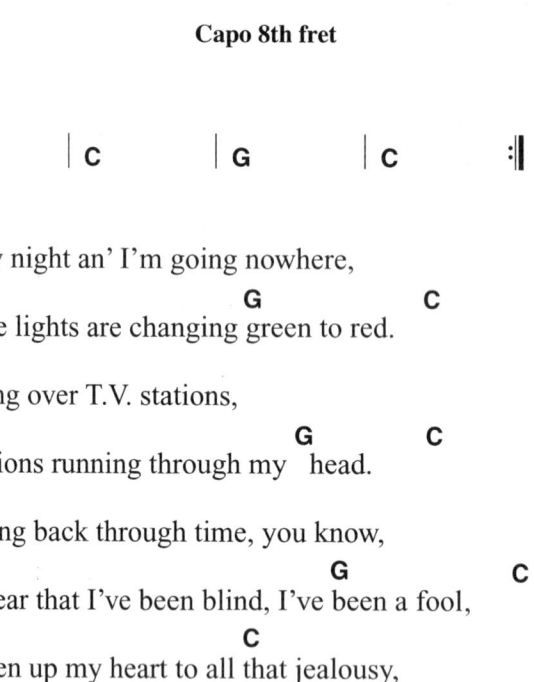

**Capo 8th fret**

*Intro*   ‖: G    | C    | G    | C    :‖

*Verse 1*
G
Friday night an' I'm going nowhere,
C                                      G              C
All the lights are changing green to red.
G
Turning over T.V. stations,
C                                         G          C
Situations running through my   head.
G
Looking back through time, you know,
    C                                 G              C
It's clear that I've been blind, I've been a fool,
     G                       C
To open up my heart to all that jealousy,
            G               C       Am
That bitterness, that ridicule.

*Verse 2*
G
Saturday I'm running wild,
      C                              G                C
An' all the lights are changin', red to green.
G
Moving through the crowds, I'm pushin',
C                                    G          C
Chemicals are rushing in my bloodstream.

© Copyright 1998 Chrysalis Music Limited.
All Rights Reserved. International Copyright Secured.

4

*cont.*

       **G**
Only wish that you were here,
                  **C**                     **G**   **C**
You know I'm seein' it so clear; I've been a - fraid,
     **G**
To show you how I really feel,
      **C**                        **G**       **C**
Ad - mit to some of those bad mis - takes I've made.

*Chorus 1*

     **G**           **D**          **Am**        **D**
And if you want it, come an' get it, for cryin' out loud.
   **G**         **D**          **Am**     **C**
The love that I was givin' you was never in doubt.
   **G**          **D**            **Am**       **D**
Let go of your heart, let go of your head, and feel it now.
   **G**          **D**            **Am**       **D**
Let go of your heart, let go of your head, and feel it now.
        **G**    **C**
Baby - lon,
        **G**    **C**
Baby - lon,
        **G**    **C**    **G**    **C**
Baby - lon.

*Verse 3*

  **G**                       **C**
Sunday, all the lights of London shining,
              **G**      **C**
Sky is fading red to blue.
**G**
Kickin' through the autumn leaves,
    **C**                          **G**     **C**
And wonderin' where it is you might be going to.
**G**
Turnin' back for home, you know,
    **C**                  **G**   **C**
I'm feeling so alone, I can't be - lieve.
**G**                      **C**
Climbin' on the stair I turn a - round,
                     **G**     **C**
To see you smiling there in front of me.

*Chorus 2*
```
            G                D              Am              D
            And if you want it,  come and get it,  for crying out loud,
            G                D              Am          C
            The love that I was  giving you was  never in  doubt.
            G               D             Am             D
            Let go of your heart, let go of your head, and feel it  now.
            G               D             Am             D
            Let go of your heart, let go of your head, and feel it  now.
```

*Chorus 3*
```
            G               D             Am             D
            Let go of your heart, let go of your head, and feel it  now.
            G               D             Am             D
            Let go of your heart, let go of your head, and feel it  now.
                    G    C
            Baby - lon,
                    G    C
            Baby - lon,
                    G    C
            Baby - lon,
                    G    C
            Baby - lon,
                    G    C    G
            Baby - lon.
```

# Early Morning Rain

Words & Music by
Gordon Lightfoot

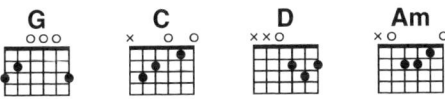

Tune guitar down by a tone

Intro      | G    | C    | D   C | G   C | G    ||

Verse 1

                      D
In the early morning rain,
       C       G    C G
With a dollar in my hand,
            C
With an achin' in my heart,
                 G    C   G
And my pockets full of sand.
             C     D
I'm a long way from home,
                G    C   G
And I miss my loved ones so,
                    D
In the early morning rain,
       C      G C   G
With no place to go.

© Copyright 1966 Moose Music, Canada.
Campbell Connelly & Company Limited.
All Rights Reserved. International Copyright Secured.

*Verse 2*

                   **D**
Out on runway number nine
      **C**         **G**   **C G**
Big seven-o-seven set to go.
                 **Am**
But I'm stuck here in the grass,
       **G**    **C G**
Where the cold wind blows.
       **C**   **D**
Now the liquor tasted good,
       **G**
And the women all were fast.
       **D**
Well there she goes my friend,
    **C**        **G**  **C**  |**D C**|**G C**|**G**  ‖
Well she's rollin' down at last.

*Verse 3*

            **D**
Hear the mighty engines roar,
    **C**     **G**   **C G**
See the silver bird on high.
        **C**
She's away and westward bound,
       **G**   **C**  **G**
Far above the clouds she'll fly,
       **C**   **D**
Where the mornin' rain don't fall,
    **G**   **C**  **G**
And the sun always shines.
      **D**
She'll be flyin' o'er my home,
   **C**       **G C**  |**D C**|**G C**|**G**  ‖
In a - bout three hours time.

*Verse 4*

                      **D**
This old airport's got me down,
  **C**                **G**  **C G**
It's no earthly good to me,
                      **Am**
'Cause I'm stuck here on the ground,
                   **G**   **C G**
As cold and drunk as I can be.
          **C**    **D**
You can't jump a jet plane,
            **G**   **C G**
Like you can a freight train.
              **D**
So I'd best be on my way,
  **C**         **G**  **C G**
In the early morning rain.
          **C**  **D**
You can't jump a jet plane
            **G**  **C G**
Like you can a freight train.
              **D**
So I'd best be on my way,
  **C**        **G**  **C**  | **D C** | **G C** | **G** ‖
In the early morning rain.

# Danger! High Voltage

Words & Music by
Tyler Spencer, Joseph Frezza, Stephen Nawara
& Anthony Selph

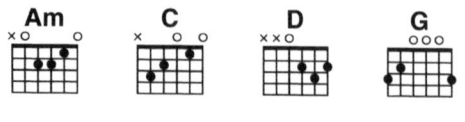

Capo 2nd fret

Intro     | Am   | Am   | Am   | Am   | Am   | Am   ||

Verse 1
**Am**                **C**
Fire in the disco,
**D**               **Am  D  G**
Fire in the taco bell.
**Am**                **C**
Fire in the disco,
**D**                 **Am      D  G**
Fire in the gates of hell.

Verse 2
**Am**                                          **C**
Don't you wanna know how we keep starting fires?
**D**                      **Am**           **D   G**
    It's my desire, it's my de - sire, it's my de - sire.
**Am**                                          **C**
Don't you wanna know how we keep starting fires?
                     **D**
    It's my de - sire, it's my desire,
**Am**       **D   G**
    It's my de - sire.

Chorus 1
**Am**            **C**
Danger, danger!   High voltage,
**D**              **Am**          **D  G**
    When we touch,     when we kiss.
**Am**            **C**
Danger, danger!   High voltage,
**D**                         **Am**           **D  G**
    When we touch, when we kiss, when we touch.

© Copyright 2002 Wall Of Sound Music.
Sony/ATV Music Publishing (UK) Limited.
All Rights Reserved. International Copyright Secured.

**Chorus 2**

Am              C
Danger, danger!   High voltage,

D              Am        D  G
  When we touch,   when we kiss.

Am              C
Danger, danger!   High voltage,

D                    Am
  When we touch, when we kiss,

        D    G
When we touch, when we (kiss).

**Guitar Solo**

                                                                         x4
‖: Am       | C        | D        | Am   D  G :‖
kiss.

**Verse 3**

    Am                                                          C
Well don't you wanna know how we keep starting fires?

D           Am         D  G
  It's my desire,   it's my de - sire.

Am                                                    C
Don't you wanna know how we keep starting fires?

D           Am         D  G
  It's my desire,   it's my de - sire.

**Chorus 3**        As Chorus 1

**Chorus 4**        As Chorus 1

**Sax Solo**       ‖: Am    | C     | D      | Am   D  G :‖

**Verse 4**

Am
Fire in the disco,

C
Fire in the disco,

D            Am   D  G
Fire in the taco bell.

Am
Fire in the disco,

C
Fire in the disco,

D              Am     D  G
Fire in the gates of hell.

**Outro**        | Am      | C       | D       | Am   D  G  |
                              The gates of hell.

              ‖: Am    | C      | D      | Am   D  G :‖
                                                               *Repeat to fade*

# Dice

Words & Music by
Finley Quaye, William Orbit & Beth Orton

Am  C  G  D

**Capo 2nd fret**

Intro    ‖: Am  | C  | G  | D  :‖  *Play 4 times*

Verse 1
    Am      C  G      D
I was crying   over you,
    Am      C  G       D
I am smiling,   I think of you.
    Am        C  G        D
Where you gardens   have no walls,
    Am                C
Breathe in the air if you care you compare,
            G   D
Don't say farewell.

Chorus 1
    Am             C
Nothing can com - pare
           G           D
To when you roll the dice and swear your love's for me.
    Am             C
Nothing can com - pare
           G           D
To when you roll the dice and swear your love's for me.

Link 1    | Am  | C  | G  | D  ‖

Verse 2
    Am      C  G      D
I was crying   over you,
    Am      C  G       D
I am smiling,   I think of you.
    Am        C  G          D
Misty mornings   and water - falls,
    Am                C
Breathe in the air if you care you compare,
            G   D
Don't say farewell.

© Copyright 2003 EMI Music Publishing Limited (66.66%)/
Rondor Music (London) Limited (33.34%).
All rights in Germany administered by Rondor Musikverlag GmbH.
All Rights Reserved. International Copyright Secured.

**Chorus 2**

Am                  C
Nothing can com - pare
                 G                  D
To when you roll the dice and swear your love's for me.
Am                  C
Nothing can com - pare
                 G                  D
To when you roll the dice and swear your love's for me.
 Am                C
(Nothing can com - pare
                 G                  D
To when you roll the dice and swear your love's for me.)

**Link 2**  | Am | C | G | D ||

**Bridge**

C
Virtuous sensibility,
G          D
  Escape ve - locity.

**Link 3**  | C | C | G | G ||

**Instrumental**  ||: Am | C | G | D :||

**Chorus 3**

Am                  C
Nothing can com - pare
                 G                  D
To when you roll the dice and you swear your love's for me.
Am                  C
Nothing can com - pare
                 G                  D
To when you roll the dice and you swear your love's for me.
Am                  C
Nothing can com - pare
                 G                  D
To when you roll the dice and you swear your love's for me.

**Coda**

Am                           C
Breathe in the air if you care you compare,
              G     D
Don't say farewell.

**Outro**  | Am | C | G | D | Am | C | G | D ||
*(Fade to end)* Nothing.

# Don't Be Cruel

Words & Music by
Otis Blackwell & Elvis Presley

G   C   Am   D

**Capo 7th fret**

*Intro*  | G | G | G | G ||

*Verse 1*
    G
You know I can be found

Sitting home all alone,
  C
If you can't come around
  G
At least please telephone.
     Am
Don't be cruel
 D       G
  To a heart that's true.

*Verse 2*
  (G)
Baby if I made you mad,

Something I might've said,
C
Please forget my past,
  G
The future looks bright ahead.
     Am
Don't be cruel
 D       G
  To a heart that's true.

*Bridge 1*
   C     D
I don't want no other lover,
  C    D      G
Baby it's still you I'm thinking of.

© Copyright 1956 Elvis Presley Music, USA.
Carlin Music Corporation.
All Rights Reserved. International Copyright Secured.

*Verse 3*

(G)
Don't stop thinking of me,

Don't make me feel this way,

C
C'mon over here and love me,

G
You know I wanted you to say

Am
Don't be cruel

D    G
 To a heart that's true.

*Bridge 2*

  C    D
Why should we be a - part?

 C   D   G
I really love you baby, cross my heart.

*Verse 4*

(G)
Let's walk up to the preacher,

And let's us say 'I do,'

C
Then you'll know you'll have me,

G
And I know that I'll have you.

Am
Don't be cruel

D    G
 To a heart that's true.

*Bridge 3*  As Bridge 1

*Tag*

Am
Don't be cruel

D    G
 To a heart that's true.

Am
Don't be cruel

D    G
 To a heart that's true.

*Outro*

  C    D
I don't want no other lover,

C   D   G
Baby it's still you I'm thinking of.

# Getting Away With It
# (All Messed Up)

Words & Music by
Tim Booth, Jim Glennie, Saul Davies,
Mark Hunter & David Baynton-Power

```
   Am           C           G           D
 x o   o      x   o  o     o o o      x x o
```

Capo 5th fret

*Intro*  | Am | Am | C | C | G | G | D | D ||

*Verse 1*
    Am          C
  Are you aching for the blade?
         G          D
That's o - kay, we're in - sured.
    Am          C
  Are you aching for the grave?
         G          D
That's o - kay, we're in - sured.

*Chorus 1*
    Am               C
  We're getting away with it all messed up,
         G                 D
Getting away with it all messed up, that's the living.
    Am               C
  We're getting away with it all messed up,
         G                 D
Getting away with it all messed up, that's the living.

*Verse 2*
    Am        C
  Daniel's saving Grace:
        G              D
She's out in deep water, hope he's a good swimmer.
    Am        C
  Daniel plays his ace
        G              D
Deep inside his temple: he knows how to surf her.

© Copyright 2001 Universal Music Publishing Limited.
All rights in Germany administered by Universal Music Publ. GmbH.
All Rights Reserved. International Copyright Secured.

**Chorus 2**

    Am                         C
We're getting away with it all messed up,
                        G               D
Getting away with it all messed up, that's the living.
    Am                         C
We're getting away with it all messed up,
                        G               D
Getting away with it all messed up, that's the living.

**Solo 1**

| Am | Am | C | C | G | G | D | D ||

**Verse 3**

    Am                C
Daniel drinks his weight,
                  G                     D
Drinks like Richard Burton, dance like John Tra - volta, now.
    Am          C
Daniel's saving Grace,
              G                    D
He was all but drowning, now they live like dolphins.

**Chorus 3**

    Am                         C
We're getting away with it all messed up,
                        G               D
Getting away with it all messed up, that's the living.
    Am                         C
We're getting away with it all messed up,
                        G               D
Getting away with it all messed up, that's the living.

**Solo 2**

| Am | Am | C | C | G | G | D | D ||

**Chorus 4**

    Am                         C
We're getting away with it (all messed up),
                        G               D
Getting away with it (all messed up), that's the living.
    Am                         C
Are we getting away with it (all messed up),
                        G               D
Getting away with it (all messed up), that's the living.
                Am
That's the living.

# Going Down

Words & Music by
John Squire & Ian Brown

G    D    C

**Capo 7th fret**

**Intro**  | G | D | C | D ||

**Verse 1**
G                      D
Dawn sings in the garden,
C                  D
Phone sings in the hall.
G                          D
This boy's dead from two days life,
        C              D
Resu - rrected by the call.

**Verse 2**
G                         D
Penny here, we've got to come,
      C             D
So come on round to me.
           G                  D
There's so much, Penny, lying here
        C          D
To touch, taste and see.

**Chorus 1**
      C              D
Ring a ding ding ding,
               G
I'm going down,
      C        G    | C    ||
   I'm coming round.

**Verse 3**
         G                D
   Penny's place, a crummy room,
        C                      D
Her Dansette crackles to Jimi's tune.
G                     D
I don't care, I taste Ambre Solaire,
        C                       D
Her neck, her thighs, her lips, her hair.

© Copyright 1989 Zomba Music Publishers Limited.
All Rights Reserved. International Copyright Secured.

18

*Chorus 2*    As Chorus 1

*Bridge 1*
   D
All thoughts of sleep desert me,
G      C
There is no time.
D                         C
Thirty minutes brings me round to
            D
Her number nine.

*Solo*    | G   | D   | C   | D   ||

*Verse 4*
G              D
Passion looks like a painting:
C          D
Jackson Pollock's number five.
    G            D
Come into the forest and taste the trees,
   C              D
The sun starts shining and I'm hard to please.

*Chorus 3*    As Chorus 1

*Bridge 2*
   D
All thoughts of sleep desert me,
G      C
There is no time.
D                         C
Thirty minutes brings me round to
            D   | G   ||
Her number nine. ―――

*Verse 5*
  C                G
So to look down on the clouds,
  C          G
You don't need to fly.
  C              D
I've never flown in a plane,
         G
I'll live until I die.

# Keep What Ya Got

**Words & Music by**
**Ian Brown & Noel Gallagher**

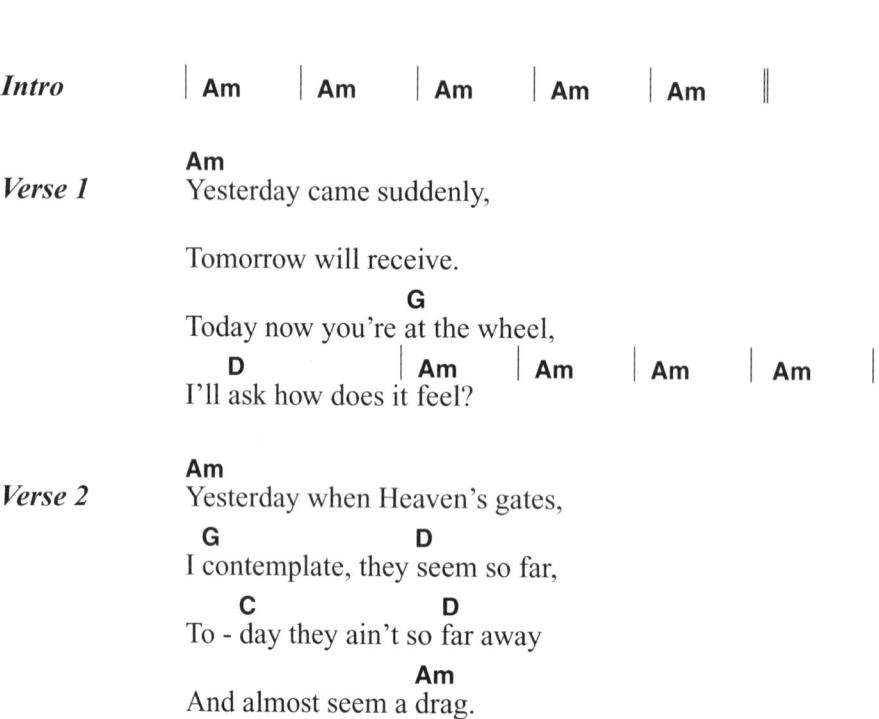

**Capo 6th fret**

*Intro*  | Am | Am | Am | Am | Am ||

*Verse 1*
    **Am**
Yesterday came suddenly,

Tomorrow will receive.
                **G**
Today now you're at the wheel,
  **D**      | **Am** | **Am** | **Am** | **Am** |
I'll ask how does it feel?

*Verse 2*
    **Am**
Yesterday when Heaven's gates,
  **G**         **D**
I contemplate, they seem so far,
    **C**           **D**
To - day they ain't so far away
                 **Am**
And almost seem a drag.

*Chorus 1*

| Am  G     | D  Am     |           |

```
Am              G      D             Am
Keep what ya got by giving it all a - way,
                G      D             Am
Keep what ya got by giving it all a - way,
G
Keep what ya got,

Hold it don't stop,
D
Keep what ya got,
              Am    | Am    | Am    | Am    ||
By giving it all a - way.
```

*Verse 3*

```
           Am
When your halo slips for good

You'll have to wear your hood.

Good to feel the breeze of fear
     G          D
On all the cynics, and you mimics,
G           D
All you losers, all abusers,
              Am    G     D          Am
Wasting all my precious en - er - gy._____
```

*Chorus 2*

```
           Am      G     D          Am
Keep what ya got, by giving it all a - way,
                G     D            Am
Keep what ya got, by giving it all a - way,
G
Keep what ya got,

Hold it don't stop,
D
Keep what ya got,
                  C
By giving it all a - way.
       D
Re - member where you came from.
```

21

***Chorus 3***

```
Am      G         D      Am
Sister she told ya on a rainy day,
                     G
They said that Heaven holds a place
    D              Am
For all of those who pray,
                        G
And if you don't believe in my dream
            D          Am
Then you don't care any - way.
             G            D         Am
Nobody or nothing's ever get - ting in your way.
```

***Chorus 4***

```
Am          G
Even as you pray the Lord
    D             Am
But don't feel you be - long,
            G             D         Am
No one's gonna notice if you're never right or wrong.
                      G
And if you and your next neighbour,
            D           Am
Yeah, you don't quite get a - long,
G
No one's gonna notice if you're singing anyway.
D
Those not coming in for free,

Well they, they've gotta pay.

 ⌢
Am
I.
```

# Maggie May

**Words & Music by
Rod Stewart & Martin Quittenton**

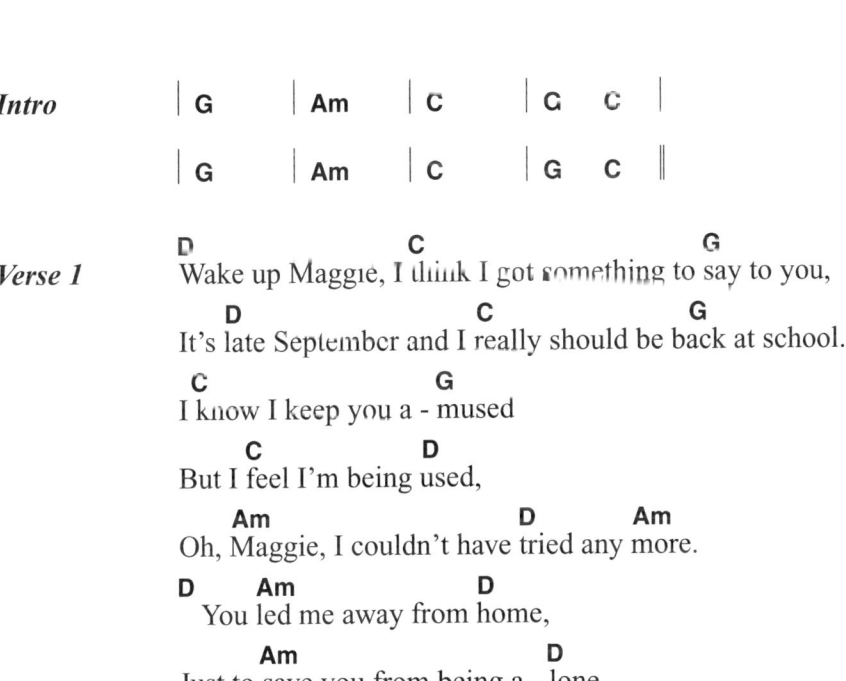

Capo 7th fret

Intro  | G | Am | C | G  C |
       | G | Am | C | G  C ||

Verse 1
    D            C                          G
Wake up Maggie, I think I got something to say to you,
    D                    C                    G
It's late September and I really should be back at school.
  C            G
I know I keep you a - mused
      C           D
But I feel I'm being used,
     Am              D     Am
Oh, Maggie, I couldn't have tried any more.
D    Am          D
  You led me away from home,
    Am               D
Just to save you from being a - lone.
   Am          D       G
You stole my heart and that's what really hurts.

© Copyright 1971 EMI Music Publishing (WP) Limited (50%)/
EMI Music Publishing Limited (37.5%)/
Warner/Chappell Music Limited (12.5%).
All Rights Reserved. International Copyright Secured.

**Verse 2**

   D       C       G
The morning sun when it's in your face really shows your age,
   D      C       G
But that don't worry me none in my eyes you're everything.
  C      G
I laughed at all of your jokes,
  C       D
My love you didn't need to coax,
  Am       D   Am
Oh, Maggie, I couldn't have tried any more.
D  Am     D
 You led me away from home,
  Am       D
Just to save you from being a - lone.
  Am       D   C  G
You stole my soul and that's a pain I can do with - out.

**Verse 3**

   D      C      G
All I needed was a friend to lend a guiding hand,
    D       C        G
But you turned into a lover and, mother, what a lover, you wore me out.
  C      G
All you did was wreck my bed
    C       D
And in the morning kick me in the head,
  Am      D   Am
Oh, Maggie, I couldn't have tried any more.
D  Am     D
 You led me away from home,
    Am      D
'Cause you didn't want to be a - lone.
  Am       D  C G
You stole my heart, I couldn't leave you if I tried.

**Instrumental** | Am  | D  | G  | C  |

         | Am  | C  | G  | G  ||

*Verse 4*

```
        D                  C                         G
I suppose I could col - lect my books and get on back to school,
        D                C                        G
Or steal my daddy's cue and make a living out of playing pool.
    C                 G
Or find myself a rock and roll band,
     C            D
That needs a helpin' hand,
       Am             D            Am
Oh, Maggie, I wished I'd never seen your face.
 D         Am              D
  You made a first class fool out of me,
        Am              D
But I'm as blind as a fool can be,
       Am           D      C   G
You stole my heart but I love you any - way.
```

*Instrumental*  | Am    | D    | G    | C    |

| Am    | C    | G    | G    ||

| Am    | D    | G    | C    |

| Am    | C    |

||: G    | Am    | C    | G    :||  *Play five times*

*Outro*

```
G          Am    C           G
Maggie I wish I'd never seen your face,
```

| G    | Am    | C    | G    |

```
G            Am   C         G
I'll get on back home   one of these days.
```

||: G    | Am    | C    | G    :||  *Repeat to fade, vocal ad lib.*

# La Bamba

Traditional
Adapted & Arranged by Ritchie Valens

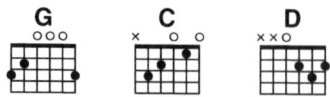

Capo 5th fret

**Intro**  | G C D | D     | G C D | D N.C. ||

**Verse 1**
```
              G         C
   Para bailar La Bamba,
     D           G           C      D          G       C
   Para bailar La Bamba, se necess - ita una poca de gracia
     D         G        C       D
   Una poca de gracia, para mi, para ti,
            G    C   D
   Ay arriba ar - riba
                G      C      D        G      C    D (N.C)
   Ay arriba ar - riba, por ti se - re, por ti sere, por ti se - re.
```

**Verse 2**
```
                G      C
   Yo no soy mari - nero,
     D           G      C      D
   Yo no soy mari - nero, soy capi - tan
           G      C    D
   Soy capi - tan, soy capi - tan,
```

**Chorus 1**
```
   G    C  D
   Bam - ba, Bamba
   G    C  D
   Bam - ba, Bamba
   G    C  D
   Bam - ba, Bamba
        G    C  D
        Bam - ba.
```

© Copyright 1958 Kemo Music Company, USA.
Carlin Music Corporation.
All Rights Reserved. International Copyright Secured.

**Verse 3**

            G     C  
Para bailar La Bamba,  
D        G       C     D        G    C  
Para bailar La Bamba, se necess - ita una poca de gracia  
D        G      C     D  
Una poca de gracia, para mi, para ti,  
           (G)  
Ay arriba ar - riba.

**Instrumental**

| G  C D | D     | G  C D | D     |
(riba.)  
||: G  C D | D     | G  C D | D     :|| *Play 4 times*

| G  C D | D     | G  C D | D N.C. ||

**Verse 4**

           G     C  
Para bailar La Bamba,  
D        G       C     D        G    C  
Para bailar La Bamba, se necess - ita una poca de gracia  
D        G      C     D  
Una poca de gracia, para mi, para ti,  
          G   C   D  
Ay arriba ar - riba  
          G    C   D      G    C    D  
Ay arriba ar - riba, por ti se - re, por ti sere, por ti se - re.

**Chorus 2**

G    C  D  
Bam - ba, Bamba  
G    C  D  
Bam - ba, Bamba  
G    C  D  
Bam - ba, Bamba  
G    C  D  
Bam - ba, Bamba

**Outro**

||: G  C D | D     | G  C D | D     :|| *Repeat to fade*

27

# Red, Red Wine

Words & Music by
Neil Diamond

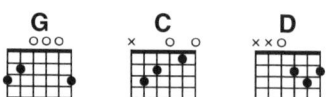

**Capo 6th fret**

*Verse 1*
     **G C**
Red, red wine,
**D C**   **G C**
Goes to my head,
**D C**    **G**   **C**
Makes me for - get that I,
**D**   **C**  **D**
Still need her so.

*Verse 2*
 **C D**  **G C**
Red, red wine,
**D** **C**  **G C**
It's up to you.
**D**  **C**  **G**    **C**
All I can do, I've done,
**D**   **C**   **D**
Mem - 'ries won't go,
**C**   **D**   **G C D**
Mem - 'ries won't go.

*Bridge 1*
 **C**   **D**   **G**
I had sworn that with time,
**C**        **G**
Thoughts of you'd leave my head.
 **D**    **G**
I was wrong; now I find
   **C**      **D**
Just one thing makes me for - get.

© Copyright 1966 Tallyrand Music Incorporated, USA.
Sony/ATV Music Publishing (UK) Limited.
All Rights Reserved. International Copyright Secured.

*Verse 3*

```
          G  C
Red, red wine,
   D    C    G    C
   Stay close to me;
   D    C    G         C
   Don't let me be alone.
   D        C    D
   It's tear - ing a - part
   C      D          (G)
   My blue, blue heart.
```

*Link 1*   | G  C  | D       | G  C  | D       |

*Bridge 2*
```
   D                  G
   I had sworn that with time,
C                          G
Thoughts of you'd leave my head.
       D         G
I was wrong; now I find
         C              D
Just one thing makes me for - get.
```

*Verse 4*
```
          G  C
Red, red wine,
   D    C    G    C
   Stay close to me;
   D    C    G         C
   Don't let me be alone.
   D        C    D
   It's tear - ing a - part
   C      D          (G)
   My blue, blue heart.
```

*Link 2*   | G  C  | D       | G  C  | D       |
                                          Red, red...

*Verse 5*
*(Fade to end)*
```
   (D)    G  C
   (Red, red) wine,
   D    C    G    C
   Stay close to me;
   D    C    G         C
   Don't let me be alone.
   D        C    D
   It's tear - ing a - part
   C      D          (G)
   My blue, blue heart.
```

# Ruby, Don't Take Your Love To Town

**Words & Music by Mel Tillis**

D    Am    G    C

Capo 5th fret

*Verse 1*

  N.C.                                                       D    Am
You've painted up your lips and rolled and curled your tinted hair,
G                     C             D
Ruby, are you contemplating going out some - where?
     C                    D                     Am
The shadows on the wall tell me the sun is going down,
    G   C   G   Am  N.C.
Oh Ru - by,_____
                            G
Don't take your love to town.

*Verse 2*

        Am                           G
For it wasn't me that started that old crazy Asia war,
      Am                  C    D
But I was proud to go and do my patriotic chores,
     C                    D         Am
And yes it's true, that I'm not the man I used to be,
    G   C   G   Am  N.C.
But Ru - by,_____
                       G
I still need some compa - ny.

© Copyright 1966 Cedarwood Publishing Company Incorporated, USA.
Universal Music Publishing Limited.
All rights in Germany administered by Universal Music Publ. GmbH.
All Rights Reserved. International Copyright Secured.

*Verse 3*

      (G)                                    C               D     Am  
It's hard to love a man whose legs are bent and para - lysed,  
      G                                   C         D  
And the wants and needs of a woman your age, Ruby, I rea - lise,  
    C                                  D                    Am  
But it won't be long, I've heard them say, un - til I'm not around,  
   G    C   G   Am  N.C.  
Oh Ru - by, _____  
                         G  
Don't take your love to town.

*Outro*

   (G)  C   G  Am  N.C.  
Oh Ru - by, _____

For God's sakes, turn around.

# Stay Another Day

**Words & Music by
Tony Mortimer, Robert Kean & Dominic Hawken**

Capo 7th fret

**Intro**      | G      | D   C   | G   D   | C      | C      ||

**Chorus 1**
      G                              D
        Baby if you've got to go a - way,
(Stay now…)
            C              G
Don't think I can take the pain,
              D          C
Won't you stay another day?
                      (Stay now…)
    G                          D
Oh, don't leave me alone like this,
        C              G
Don't you say it's the final kiss,
                    (Stay now…)
             D        C
Won't you stay another day?
                    (Stay now…)

**Verse 1**
    G                         D   C
Don't you know we've come to far now,
    G         D           C
Just to go  and try to throw it all a - way.
G                    D   C
Thought I heard you say you love me,
         G         D       C
That you love was gonna be  here to stay.
G                  D   C
I've only just begun to know you,
           G          D          C
All I can say is won't you stay just one more day?

© Copyright 1994 Porky Publishing/Bandmodel Limited.
Universal Music Publishing Limited.
All rights in Germany administered by Universal Music Publ. GmbH.
All Rights Reserved. International Copyright Secured.

*Chorus 2*     As Chorus 1

*Verse 2*
```
           G                    D       C
    I touch your face while you are sleep - ing,
                   G             D              C
     And hold you hand, don't under - stand what's going on.
     G                      D      C
       Good times we had return to haunt me,
                    G            D              C
     Though it's for you, all that I do seems to be wrong.
```

*Chorus 3*     As Chorus 1

*Chorus 4*
*(Fade out during chorus)*
```
       G                         D
        Baby if you've got to go a - way,
         C              G
     Don't think I can take the pain,
             D            C
     Won't you stay another day?
                             (Stay now...)
       G                      D
        Oh, don't leave me alone like this,
              C              G
     Don't you say it's the final kiss,
                             (Stay now...)
             D           C
     Won't you stay another day?
                             (Stay now...)
```

# Sunday Morning

**Words & Music by**
Adam Levine, James Valentine, Jesse Carmichael,
Mickey Madden & Ryan Dusick

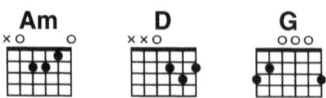

Capo 5th fret

**Intro**
```
        Drums
          4
| |---------| ||

|Am    |D   |G    |Am    |D   |G    ||
        (Yeah.)
```

**Verse 1**
    Am     D       G
Sunday morning, rain is falling.
    Am     D       G
Steal some covers share some skin.
    Am     D       G
Clouds are shrouding us in moments unforgettable.
     Am     D        G
You twist to fit the mould that I am in.

**Bridge 1**
     Am       D       G
But things just get so crazy, living life gets hard to do.
       Am       D       G
And I would gladly hit the road, get up and go if I knew
     Am       D       G
That someday it would lead me back to you,
     Am       D       G
That someday it would lead me back to you.

**Chorus 1**
              Am  D  G
That may be all   I    need.
                      Am  D  G
In darkness she is all   I    see.
                      Am   D  G
Come and rest your bones   with  me.
                              Am
Driving slow on Sunday morning,
             D     G
And I never want to leave.

© Copyright 2002 February Twenty Second Music, USA.
Universal Music Publishing MGB Limited.
All Rights in Germany Administered by Musik Edition Discoton GmbH
(A Division of Universal Music Publishing Group)
All Rights Reserved. International Copyright Secured.

**Verse 2**
```
        Am       D              G
    Fingers trace your ev'ry outline, oh yeah.
        Am       D              G
    Paint a picture with my hands, oh, woah.
        Am       D              G
    Back and forth we sway like branches in a storm.
              Am             D                G
    Change the weather, still to - gether when it ends.__
```

**Chorus 2**   As Chorus 1

**Breakdown**
```
                Instrumental (N.C.)
                       14
         |  |—————————————————|  ||
```

**Bridge 2**
```
            Am              D              G
    But if things just get so crazy, living life gets hard to do.
             Am              D                G
    Sunday morning, rain is falling and I'm calling out to you,
             Am           D            G
    Singing someday it will bring me back to you,
             Am         D              G
    Find a way to bring my - self back home to you.

    You may not know…
```

**Chorus 3**
```
                  Am  D   G
    ||: That may be all  I   need.
                    Am  D  G
    In darkness she is all  I   see.
                      Am    D   G
    Come and rest your bones with  me.
                          Am
    Driving slow on Sunday morning,
           D         G
    And I never want_ to leave. :||  Repeat ad lib. to fade
```

35

# Sweetest Thing

Words & Music by
U2

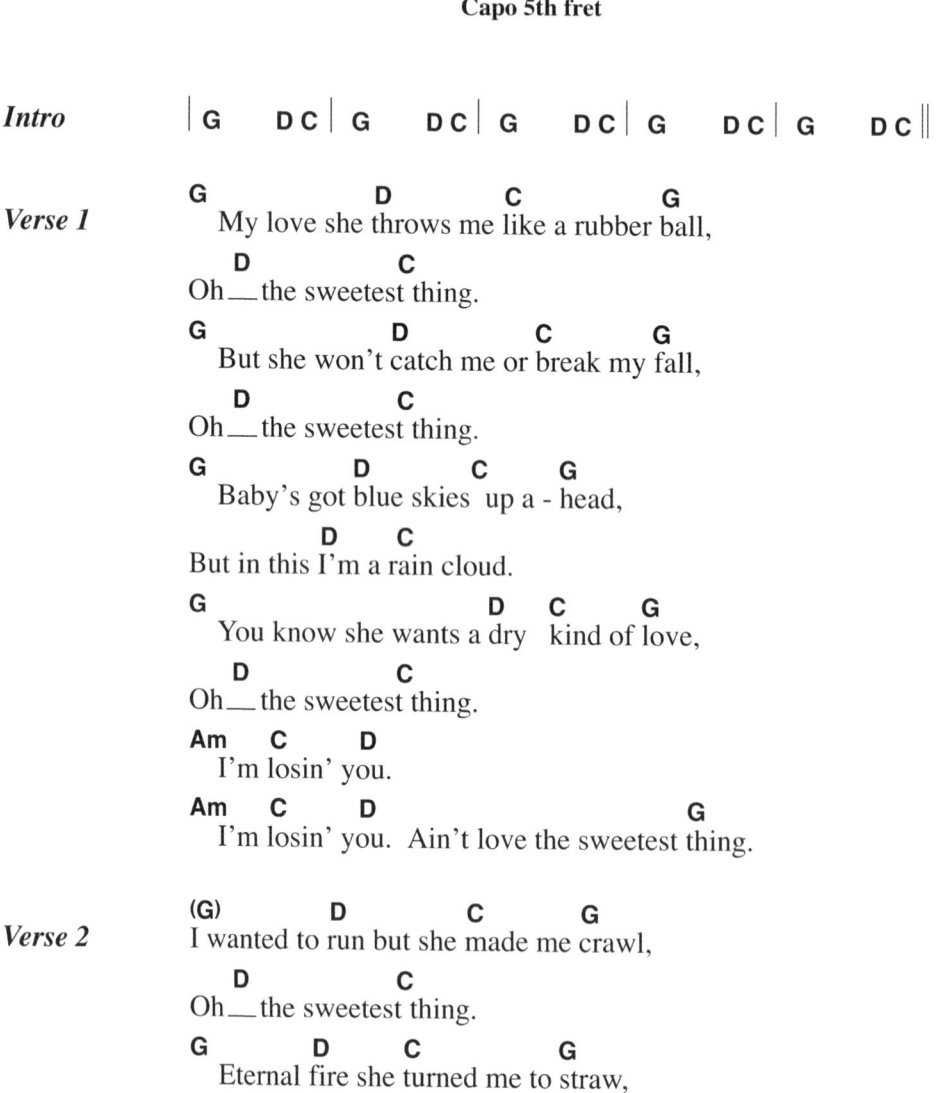

**Capo 5th fret**

**Intro**  | G   D C | G   D C | G   D C | G   D C | G   D C ||

**Verse 1**
G          D         C         G
My love she throws me like a rubber ball,
    D         C
Oh—the sweetest thing.
G           D            C         G
But she won't catch me or break my fall,
    D         C
Oh—the sweetest thing.
G         D          C    G
Baby's got blue skies up a - head,
      D        C
But in this I'm a rain cloud.
G                   D    C     G
You know she wants a dry kind of love,
    D         C
Oh—the sweetest thing.
Am    C    D
I'm losin' you.
Am    C    D                           G
I'm losin' you. Ain't love the sweetest thing.

**Verse 2**
(G)       D        C        G
I wanted to run but she made me crawl,
    D         C
Oh—the sweetest thing.
G         D      C         G
Eternal fire she turned me to straw,
    D         C
Oh—the sweetest thing.

© Copyright 1987 Blue Mountain Music Limited/Mother Music Limited/
PolyGram International Music Publishing B.V.
All rights in Germany administered by Universal Music Publ. GmbH.
All Rights Reserved. International Copyright Secured.

*cont.*

```
        G          D      C
     I know I got black eyes,
           G          D        C
But they burn so brightly for her.
  G          D     C      G
    I guess it's a blind kind of love.
         D            C
Oh ___ the sweetest thing.
Am    C    D
   I'm losin' you, whoa,
Am    C    D
I'm   losin' you.
                       C
Ain't love the swee - test thing?
```

Ain't love the sweetest thing?

*Instrumental*   ‖: G    D C | G    D C | G    D C :‖
*w/ vocal ad lib.*

*Verse 3*
```
       G        D     C         G
    Blue eyed boy to brown eyed girl,
      D         C
Oh ___ the sweetest thing.
  G           D      C              G
    You can set it up, but you still see the tear,
      D         C
Oh ___ the sweetest thing.
  G         D      C         G
    Baby's got blue skies up a-head,
            D      C
But in this I'm a rain cloud,
  G          D    C       G
    Ours is a stormy kind of love,
      D         C
Oh ___ the sweetest thing.
```

*Outro*
```
     G              C
 ‖: Do do do do, do do do do,
 G           C
Do, do do do do do do do.   :‖
 G           C
Do do do do, do the sweetest thing.
 G           C                  G
Do do do do, do the sweetest thing.
```

37

# So Young

**Words & Music by
Andrea Corr, Caroline Corr, Sharon Corr & Jim Corr**

G   C   D   Am

Intro
       G         C          D
Yeah, yeah, yeah, yeah, yeah.
       G         C          D
Yeah, yeah, yeah, yeah, yeah.

Verse 1
               G
We are taking it easy.
 C             D
Bright and breezy, yeah.
           G
We are living it up
 C              D
Just fine and dandy, yeah.

Pre-chorus 1
       Am                     C   D
And it really doesn't matter that we don't eat,
       Am                    C   D
And it really doesn't matter if we never sleep,
      Am
No, it really doesn't matter.
 C              D
Really doesn't matter at all.

© Copyright 1997 Universal-Songs Of PolyGram International Incorporated/
Beacon Communications Music Company, USA.
Universal Music Publishing Limited.
All rights in Germany administered by Universal Music Publ. GmbH.
All Rights Reserved. International Copyright Secured.

|              | G |
|---|---|
| ***Chorus 1*** | 'Cause we are so young now, |

           C                      D
We are so young, so young now.
                G
And when to - morrow comes
     C         D
We can do it all a - gain.

             G
***Verse 2***     We are chasing the moon,
      C          D
Just running wild and free.
       G
We are following through
   C          D
Every dream and every need.

           Am                     C    D
***Pre-chorus 2*** And it really doesn't matter that we don't eat,
          Am                    C    D
And it really doesn't matter if we never sleep,
      Am
No, it really doesn't matter.
C           D
Really doesn't matter at all.

            G
***Chorus 2***   'Cause we are so young now,
     C               D
We are so young, so young now.
              G
And when to - morrow comes
   C        D
We can do it all a - gain.

*Chorus 3*

        **G**
Yeah, we're so young now,
     **C**           **D**
We are so young, so young now.
               **G**
And when to - morrow comes
    **C**          **D**
We'll just do it all a - gain.

*Bridge*

       **Am**   **C**     **D**
All a - gain,    all a - gain, he-yeah.
       **Am**   **C**     **D**
All a - gain,    all a - gain,____yeah, yeah, yeah.

*Chorus 4*

**G**
So young now,
     **C**           **D**
We are so young, so young now.
               **G**
And when to - morrow comes
    **C**          **D**
We'll just do it all a - gain.

*Chorus 5*     As Chorus 3

*Coda*

             **G**          **C**         **D**
‖: We are so young_____ yeah!
                (yeah, yeah, yeah, yeah)
        **G**          **C**         **D**
We are so young_____ yeah! :‖   *Repeat to fade*
         (yeah, yeah, yeah, yeah)

# Turn

**Words & Music by Fran Healy**

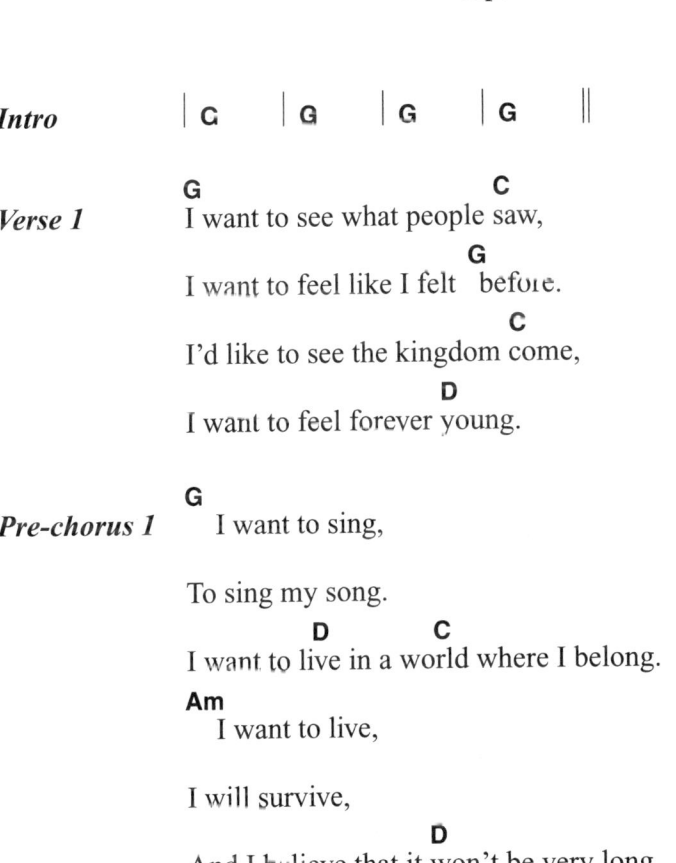

**Capo 9th fret**

*Intro*  | G | G | G | G ||

*Verse 1*
```
    G                        C
I want to see what people saw,
                         G
I want to feel like I felt before.
                             C
I'd like to see the kingdom come,
                     D
I want to feel forever young.
```

*Pre-chorus 1*
```
         G
    I want to sing,

To sing my song.
            D            C
I want to live in a world where I belong.
Am
   I want to live,

I will survive,
                        D
And I believe that it won't be very long.
```

© Copyright 1999 Sony/ATV Music Publishing (UK) Limited.
All Rights Reserved. International Copyright Secured.

**Chorus 1**

      C        D
If we turn, turn, ___
  G      C
Turn, turn, turn.
          D     G
Turn, turn, ___ turn. ___
    C       D
If we turn, turn, ___
  G      C
Turn, turn, turn.
                D      G
Then we might learn, ___ learn. ___

**Verse 2**

  (G)
   So where's the stars?
     C
Up in the sky.

And what's the moon?
      G
A big bal - loon.
                  C
We'll never know unless we grow,
                       D
There's so much world outside the door.

**Pre-chorus 2**

G
  I want to sing,

To sing my song.
          D       C
I want to live in a world where I'll be strong.
**Am**
  I want to live,

I will survive,
                 D
And I believe that it won't be very long.

**Chorus 2**

```
          C            D
If we turn, turn, ____
     G          C
Turn, turn, turn.
              D        G
Turn, turn, ____ turn. ____
          C            D
If we turn, turn, ____
     G          C
Turn, turn, turn.
                  C    D       G
Then we might learn, ____ learn.
```

**Link**

```
   D
      We've got to turn, we've got to turn.

| C   D  | G   C  | C   D  | G        ||
```

**Chorus 3**

```
          C            D
If we turn, turn, ____
     G          C
Turn, turn, turn.
              D        G
Turn, turn, ____ turn. ____
          C            D
If we turn, turn, ____
     G          C
Turn, turn, turn.
                  C
Then we might learn,
             D        G
Learn to turn. _____
```

**Coda**

```
||: G    | G    | G    | G    :||
```

43

# Walk Of Life

Words & Music by
Mark Knopfler

G   D   Am   C

**Capo 9th fret**

**Intro**    | (G)    | (C)    | (D)    | (C)  (D) |

  ||: G    | C    | D    | C  D  :||   *Play 4 times*

**Verse 1**
G
Here comes Johnny singing oldies, goldies;

'Be-Bop-A-Lula', 'Baby What I Say',

Here comes Johnny singing 'I Got A Woman',

Down in the tunnels, trying to make it pay.

**Pre-chorus 1**
　　C
　 He got the action, he got the motion,
G
　 Oh yeah, the boy can play.
　　C
　 Dedication, devotion,
G
Turning all the night time into the day.

**Chorus 1**
　　　　(G)　　　　　　　　　D
He do the song about the sweet-lovin' woman,
　　　　　　　G　　　　　　C
He do the song about the knife,
　　　　　　G　　D　　　　C　Am
He do the walk,　do the walk of life,
D
Yeah, he do the walk of (life.)

**Link 1**    | G    | C    | D    | C  D  ||
              life.

© Copyright 1985 Chariscourt Limited.
Straitjacket Songs Limited.
All Rights Reserved. International Copyright Secured.

**Verse 2**

G
Here comes Johnny and he'll tell you the story,

Hand me down my walkin' shoes,

Here come Johnny with the power and the glory,

Backbeat, the talkin' blues.

**Pre-chorus 2**

C
He got the action, he got the motion,
G
Yeah the boy can play.
C
Dedication, devotion,
G
Turning all the night time into the day.

**Chorus 2**

             G                  D
He do the song about the sweet-lovin' woman,
            G              C
He do the song about the knife,
        G   D         C   Am
He do the walk, do the walk of life,
D
Yeah, he do the walk of (life.)

**Link 2**

‖: G  | C  | D  | C  D  :‖
   life.

**Verse 3**     As Verse 1

**Pre-chorus 3**   As Pre-chorus 1

**Chorus 3**

         G                 D
And after all the violence and double-talk,
             G                 C
There's just a song in all the trouble and the strife.
         G   D             C   Am
You do the walk, yeah you do the walk of life,
D
Hmm, you do the walk of (life.)

**Coda**

‖: G  | C  | D  | C  D  :‖ *Repeat to fade*
   life.

# Woodstock

Words & Music by
Joni Mitchell

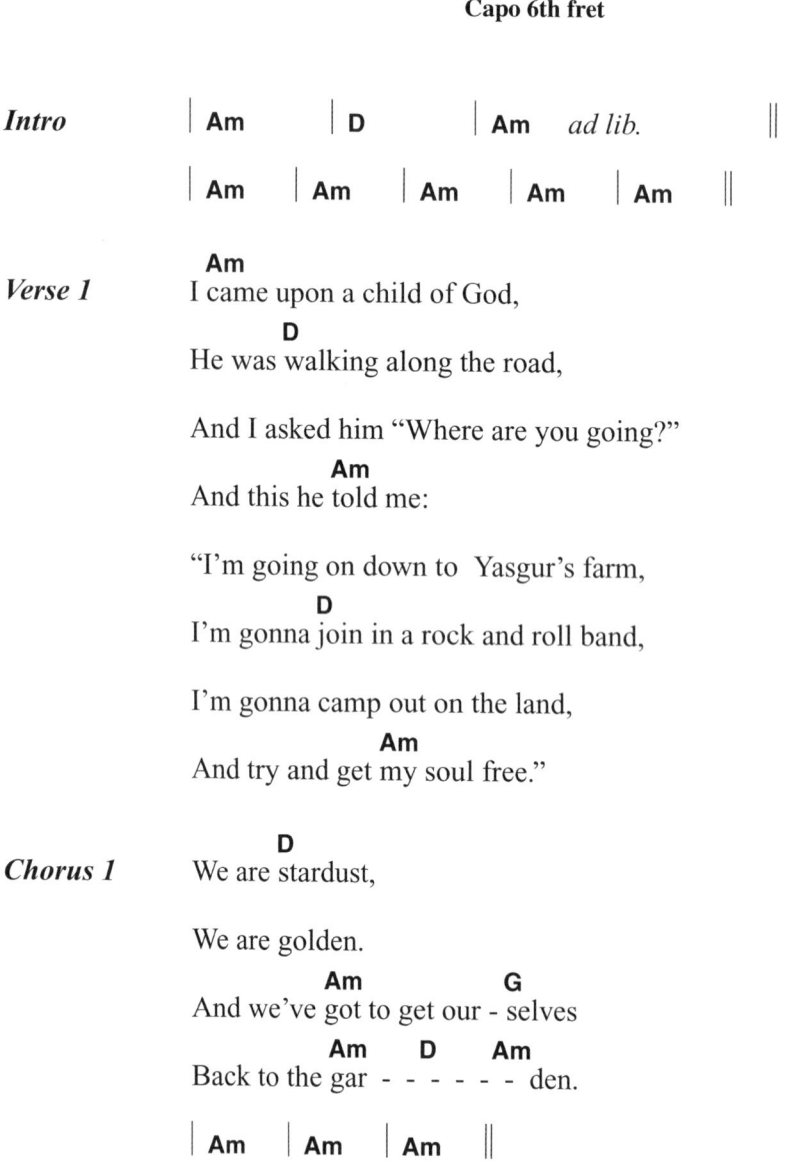

Capo 6th fret

**Intro**  | Am     | D     | Am   *ad lib.*   ||
         | Am  | Am  | Am  | Am  | Am  ||

**Verse 1**
    **Am**
I came upon a child of God,
  **D**
He was walking along the road,

And I asked him "Where are you going?"
          **Am**
And this he told me:

"I'm going on down to Yasgur's farm,
     **D**
I'm gonna join in a rock and roll band,

I'm gonna camp out on the land,
             **Am**
And try and get my soul free."

**Chorus 1**
    **D**
We are stardust,

We are golden.
       **Am**        **G**
And we've got to get our - selves
       **Am**  **D**  **Am**
Back to the gar - - - - - - den.

| Am  | Am  | Am  ||

© Copyright 1969 Crazy Crow Music, USA.
Sony/ATV Music Publishing (UK) Limited.
All Rights Reserved. International Copyright Secured.

*Verse 2*

    **Am**
Then can I walk beside you,

        **D**
I have come here to lose the smog,

And I feel to be a cog
  **Am**
In — something turning.

Well, maybe it is just the time of year,
    **D**
Or maybe it's the time of man,

And I don't know who I am
          **Am**
But you know life is for learning.

*Chorus 2*

    **D**
We are stardust,

We are golden,
      **Am**        **G**
And we've got to get our - selves
      **Am**  **D**  **Am**
Back to the gar - - - - - - den.

| Am | Am | Am ||

*Verse 3*

  **Am**
By the time we got to Woodstock,
  **D**
We were half a million strong,

And everywhere there was
  **Am**
Song and celebration.

And I dreamed I saw the bombers
  **D**
Riding shotgun in the sky,

And they were turning into butterflies
  **Am**
A - bove our nation.

***Chorus 3***          **D**
We are stardust,

Million year old carbon.

We are golden,

Caught in the Devil's bargain,
         **Am**         **G**
And we've got to get our - selves
      **D**    **C**   **Am**    | **Am**   ||
Back to the gar - - - - - - den.

***Outro***      | **Am**    | **D**    | **Am**    | **Am**    |

||: **Am**    | **Am**    | **D**    | **D**    :||
*With vocal ad lib.*

| **Am**    | **D**    | **Am**    | **D**    |

| **Am**    | **Am**    | **Am**    | **Am**    |

| **Am**    | **D**    | **D**    | **Am**    ||